Hello! <u>Before you start reading,</u> I want to mention that these poems were written during a difficult time for me, I was struggling with my mental health and felt very alone. If you are struggling with your mental health, there is a page of helplines and mental health charities at the back of the book, please contact them.

There are not many happy poems in the book, however, I think this is really important. When I was struggling (and I still am) I would read inspirational poems, and it would mean nothing, if anything it would make me feel number than I already was. It was by reading poems, that were written from the point of view of a 'messed up' mind, that made me realise I wasn't alone. I think that is more important than anything. You can dream and plan for a healthy, happy future, but that's no good if you're struggling in the present. That's the biggest thing I've learned, help yourself now, a self-help plan only works if you follow through.

<u>A few things I should mention:</u>

-at the back of the book, there is room for your own poems and notes, it is a beautiful thing for people to write alongside another, even if not in person but on a page of a book!

-some poems speak of my eating disorder, there is a page at the back of the book which outlines what my eating disorder is, I recommend you read that page before you begin reading.

-although I do not have my own diary that I write in, feel free to use this book as your own diary, my poems tell my story of self-discovery (and in some poems, a lack of). I call poetry my free therapy, I write what I write, I don't think too much about it, I hope you do the same.

-lastly, if you are interested in poetry, whether you want to write, or do write, at the back of the book is a page with the names of the poetry books I have been collecting from some amazing poets, I recommend all of them to writers.

On that note, feel free to flick the page and start reading! Hopefully, we can meet again in my next book!

-Lola xx

'My mother told me to be a lady. And for her, that meant be your own person, be independent'.

- Ruth Bader Ginsburg

-I write my words in protest,

Since, still, after hundreds of years,

We only have limited rights.

We will have no rest,

We will wipe away our tears,

And we will finally end the fight.

Nothing for us will be prohibited,

We will stand triumphantly,

And with our mothers and sisters and daughters
by our side,

We will win the war,

It will be nothing like they've seen before,

We will stand united,

With our shields, swords, and scars,

We will break through the bars,

No longer caged we will be free.

We will be free to live,

And we will be free to breathe,

With our hearts on our sleeves,

We would have done it for them,

The next generation,

The new women.

The free women.

-We are told, as girls, to care about pink, dresses and dolls,

But frankly, I don't care about of any of that.

I care about the ink that bleeds when I over share in my rhyming words,

If I am a girl, does that mean I have to stop scribbling letters,

Or typing stanzas on my phone,

Because I am told I should be standing near the King on his throne,

Because I should do what I'm asked,

Ginerly sitting with my legs crossed,

Like a pin holding a picture,

Because that is all I am,

That is all we are as women,

As girls,

We are told, if not by ourselves,

By our society,

To sit and smile zealously next to the man with whom we share the other ring,

We are just pins, holding our Kings, all the same on display,

Making their reputation pristine.

But I want my own throne on display,

At the highest point of the tallest mountain

For all of the Kingdom to see,

I will wear my crown with pride and confidence,

Because no man is needed for my stability.

So why don't you stand, smiling zealously,

While I raise my crown above me.

-We were in our school uniforms,

When were winked at.

We were in our school uniforms,

When we were whistled at.

We were in our school uniforms,

When we were followed.

Both times.

I was in my school uniform when I was pushed,

And shoved against a broken fence,

And I was in my uniform when I was
'complimented' on my 'nice cherries'.

And it is in my school uniform, when I worry if
today is the day I'll become a part of the statist

-Rape culture is more than its meaning,

When we can still see the glass ceiling.

-Let's end this with us,

In our generation,

I don't want my children to suffer,

For them it will be tougher.

Before rape loses its meaning, we need to break through the glass ceiling,

Before we are caged in the stereotypes we try to escape.

Women are women,

Not objects for you to mock,

Break,

And manipulate,

We are life givers,

We are beautiful glass figures,

Goddesses who earn and learn,

Who teach and preach our rights to live.

But there's a problem,

I am too scared to look in the mirror,

And I know I'm not the only one,

Our beautiful goddess figures,

Are named and shamed,

Battered and bruised,

Words paint their selves onto our skin,

We overeat and undereat,

Because our bodies and minds are constantly beaten by the men who restrict us,

And limit us,

We need to win this battle for the next generation of girls,

They need to know their beauty, their worth,

How they are each rare pearls,

I want them to have a life,

To live,

Not just exist.

'If not me, Who? If not now, When?'

-Emma Watson

-A ballerina in a music box,

Like a girl in the modern day,

Locked away in a wooden box,

More like societal categories,

Sealed with locks.

-I do not want to grow up in a world,

Where my personality is compacted,

And I have to cover up my skin,

In case the boys are distracted.

I don't want to be raised in a patriarchy,

Where misogyny is accepted,

And the world is full of men preaching hypocrisy,

No, I do not hate men,

But when they point, laugh and rate *'her'* out of ten,

I cannot help the urge to scream the statistics,

At the men who claim it is not them.

-To my daughter (if I ever meet you),

I promise, I will try to make you less like me.

Less insecure,

And lonely.

I will make sure that along with calling you pretty,

I call you pretty clever,

And intelligent,

Pretty strong,

And determined,

Pretty independent,

And hard-working,

Pretty amazing,

And brilliant,

I will make sure you know your worth,

From the second our eyes meet.

I will make sure you understand who you are,

And support you when you don't.

I will make sure that you are self-reliant enough to pick yourself up,

And dependant on others enough that you always feel loved.

I will make sure you are in touch with your passions,

And thrive in your strengths,

But always have resilience with your weaknesses.

I will make sure you have self-love,

And self-respect,

I will make sure of that more than anything else.

I will make sure that all your intelligence,

Strength,

Determination,

Independence,

And brilliance,

Is so apparent within you,

That people are in awe.

I will love you unconditionally,

And I will make sure you know it.

But most importantly,

I will make sure you love yourself unconditionally.

And I will make sure that you know self-love is the most important kind of love.

Dear daughter,

You are amazing.

-What is femininity?

Well for me,

No layer of makeup,

Or writing a song about a breakup

Can begin to explain the generational pain,

Or the fear when the night sky is not clear,

Is my 'girly innocence' will be taken by a man's wickedness.

None of this is what I want to reminisce when I'm with my granddaughter,

Because I don't want another girl's childhood made shorter.

What is femininity?

A question with great power,

Because being a woman isn't being a pretty flower in bloom,

Or the sweet smell of your favourite perfume,

And being a girl isn't playing with dolls,

Or trying on nice dresses,

Try avoiding internet trolls

And not feeling congratulated for your own successes,

Because if you're not a boy playing football,

What's the point of feeling anything but small?

What is femininity?

I often think people's ignorance takes over

Because they give history the cold shoulder,

They choose to forget the Suffragette's silhouette,

And Emeline Pankhurst,

But when will the bubble burst?

Every year on international women's day,

There is at least one boy or man that has to say,

'Why is there not an international man's day?'

Well sir, is the past a blur,

Because to my knowledge,

Men did not have the courage to stand up for girls and women,

Or did they just turn a blind eye,

Act shy to what's real,

Make up the rules

Say women are their' crown jewels',

When they treat us like dust and make the girls mistrust.

What is femininity?

This will not be the final time

Because I feel that no definition is mine,

Throughout history, femininity has changed,

Making it a complete mystery.

For me, femininity is not domestic or biblical,

For me femininity does not stem from the apple tree,

Because not every woman is like Eve,

So curious and naïve,

And for me, femininity is not being a Lady Macbeth,

Because not every woman is manipulative and plans their own partners last breathe.

So, if you were to ask me,

'What is femininity?'

I could not give you a straight answer,

Because when speaking about femininity,

It is whatever we women want it to be.

The Statistics

-There are 3.4 million female victims of sexual assault in the UK.

-5/6 people did not report their assault.

-There are 631,000 male victims of sexual assault in the UK.

-80% of women have been harassed.

-73% of adolescents who self-harm are girls.

-700,000 people in the UK have eating disorders, 90% of them are girls.

If you or someone you know are a victim of sexual assault, harassment or violence of some kind, never be afraid to reach out. You are not alone.

If you self-harm or have thoughts of suicide, you are not alone. Reach out.

You are not alone.

Reach out! Here are some charities to contact:

-The National Child Traumatic Stress Network (NCTSN)

-Rape Abuse and Incest National Network (RAINN)

-Call your countries emergency helping (UK-999)

'Feminism is about gender equality not women superiority'

-Meagan Russon

-I don't know who you are yet,

And I don't know if I believe in soulmates or love at first sight,

But either way, I hope that you are special enough to write a poem about.

I hope that your eyes are special enough for me to make them rhyme,

And I hope that your voice is so heavenly,

I become hypnotised,

That you are such a warm and welcoming person,

That I have no choice but to write about you,

Or even better,

For you.

I hope you appreciate me.

My talents,

And intelligence,

I hope that you remind me of my talents,

And intelligence,

I hope you appreciate everything about me,

Because I know I will appreciate everything about you.

I hope you know me better than I know myself,

And I hope that you support me,

And are by my side for everything,

No matter how cringey it sounds.

I hope that you respect me,

And treat me kindly,

And of course, with love.

I hope you love me.

I hope that we are compatible,

No matter our 'star signs',

I hope you make me laugh,

I hope that I can never stay annoyed at you,

And I hope you know all of my insecurities,

And I hope you know how to chase them all
away.

I hope you know yourself too.

I hope you are the sun that melts away my
worries and anxiety,

But, most importantly,

I hope you love and accept every part of me,

Physically and mentally,

We know I can't offer that for myself,

I hope you love me.

I hope you are special enough to write about.

-I hope that when I meet you,

It isn't love at first sight,

I want to learn to love you.

I want to live the life of the girl in the film,

To lay by the fire with you,

As the sparks consume us,

We sit in silence,

Listening to the roar of flames,

And the united beating of our hearts.

I hope that when you look at me, time freezes,

So that I can embrace the beauty of your eyes,

And every feature of your face that makes you perfect.

I hope that when we say 'I love you' for the first time,

We are half asleep in bed,

Or watching a film together,

Cosy on the sofa,

It is the little things that mean the most.

I hope that every second we spend with each other,

We do not think a thing,

We are just happy and grateful to be together,

I hope that the smallest things make the biggest memories,

All I want to remember is being in love and happy with you,

And for you to feel the same way too,

And I want to remember every time we say 'I love you'.

I just really hope that all of this comes true.

-I don't think you realise how much it affects me.

My eating disorder.

You don't know of the countless times I burst into tears,

Because unless I sort myself out, I'm gonna be stuck like this forever,

How will someone ever love me if I can't control my senses,

And their meltdowns?

I don't think you understand either.

I don't really think you try to understand.

Food is one of the things that keeps us alive,

That keeps everyone alive,

Imagine not being able to look at food,

Without having to stop yourself from breaking down,

To smell it when your mind thinks the fumes could kill you,

To talk about or think about food, without drowning in your own tears,

Imagine feeling like this for years,

Not even remembering feeling or being 'normal'.

The worst thing about ARFID,

Wherever you go,

Whatever you do,

Food is always going to follow,

Because it has to,

No matter how well you hide,

Or how far your run,

It always catches up to you.

-Mum, I'm so sorry. I never realised how wrong I was. You booked the appointments. And listened to me cry until my eyes ran dry, you took me to the appointments. Are you struggling too? In my selfishness, it never crossed my mind how much all of this could affect someone else. I knew this would be difficult for you, but I never imagined what you could be feeling. What I said was true though. I didn't feel supported by you, or heard, or seen, but I guess I was being too mean. I know your idea of support is different from mine, but I just never feel listened to, so, I don't tell you when I cry anymore, not normally. But I'm crying as I write this for you, knowing full well that I'll never be brave enough to give it to you. And knowing full well that you won't read this book. I am so sorry. For everything. I have been caught up in my own shame and confusion and insecurities, that I never thought about how much this might be affecting you. I'm so sorry.

-I usually refer to my eating disorder as 'It',

It scares me to call It by It's name,

Shocks me into remembering I have it.

I try to hide from It.

I try to run from It.

I especially don't like using It's full name,

My mind assesses which words resonate with me,

Isolates me for the words that don't,

And isolates me, more so, for the words that do.

I don't like to admit it,

But I'm scared of It.

I've had It for so long,

But it's only now that I know,

How long have I been under the spell of It?

Barricaded behind It's control?

-You cannot change the past,

I am not holding a grudge,

I am holding memories,

Memories that impacted me,

Memories that changed me.

Memories that shaped me.

-I don't know how this all started.

This is not like anorexia or bulimia,

This did not become from body image and insecurities.

If anything,

It has made my body image and insecurities worse.

No one can pin point its origin.

Not me.

I wish I could.

Find out why I am like this.

Find out whether I first resonated with the A, R, F I or D.

It is all a mystery.

-I'm not ill enough to get help.

To summarise what she said to me.

The dietician.

The professional.

If my eating disorder limited me to a couple less foods,

I would receive the help I need.

Because I'm not skinny,

I have not been referred.

She wants to deal with my weight first.

My weight doesn't control my diet,

My ARFID does.

My weight doesn't make me gag and feel sick at the sight of food,

My ARFID does.

Me weight didn't cause my lack of iron,

My ARFID did.

So why are you ignoring it?

I sat in front of you and cried,

I cried uncontrollably.

With puffy eyes,

A beating chest,

And drowned sleeves from their attempt to comfort my eyes.

You told me I am not sick enough to get the help I need.

I help I have needed for the majority of my life,

And the help I have craved and prepared myself for over the last year.

You tell me I am not sick enough as I drown in the sadness of my own soul.

When I lose weight, I can get help.

And even then it wont be the help I need.

Binging is the only thing that keep me from hurting myself.

But I am not sick enough to get help.

-I'm finding it really hard to come to terms with my eating disorder,

Which when I think about it is quite strange,

I don't remember not having it.

Its only because I've been diagnosed that it feels wrong.

But the weirdest feeling,

Is knowing that now, I can get help.

That, after all of this time,

All of these years, living in the dark,

I can see a light.

'The more I like me, the less I want to pretend to be other people'

-Jamie Lee Curtis

-I am so envious of you.

Your perfectly shaped face,

And jawline,

Your cute button nose,

And the beautiful shine that surrounds you,

You are like a magnet for the sun,

You obtain a never-dimming glow.

The earthly tone to your eyes,

They reflect mother nature herself,

You hold the power of the earth in your hands.

The curve of your hips,

And dip of your waist,

The flatness of your tummy,

The way your hair so warmly lays on your shoulders,

Like a siren's spell,

Your beauty hypnotises me.

Your strength,

And independence,

I truly cannot decide whether your personality or appearance is more beautiful.

I am so envious of you.

-I know I am more than the thoughts about being thin,

Than the belly I fail to hide in my trousers,

And the wrappers in the bin.

I know I am more than the endless amount of clothes I've demolished from where my thighs chafe.

And I know I am more than the monstrous figure I see when I look in the mirror.

But no matter how much I know,

I never feel like I am.

-How to be prettier

How to be beautiful

How to be pretty

How to lose weight

How to lose weight fast

How to lose weight quickly

Quick ways to lose weight

How to be skinny

How to lose weight in a week

How to look better in my school uniform

How to be thinner

How to have a skinny body

How to have a skinny waist

How to use makeup

How to look good

'You're a human being, you live once and life is so wonderful, so eat that damn red velvet cupcake'

-Emma Stone

-Isolation is not freeing,

I want to spread my wings and start seeing,

But every time you make a sound,

My soul takes offence,

I can't help it, it's become my defence,

I'm used to words feeling like an arrow to the core,

So, I'm sorry, but your words are like a tsunami,

And I stand at the shore,

Waiting to be consumed by your evil,

When in reality,

It is not yours, but my minds upheaval.

-Yes.

I am struggling.

I don't understand your disbelief.

-I told you

'I don't want to be here anymore'

You asked if I was talking about the school building or earth,

You asked me if I have *those kind of thoughts*

Nervously laughing,

I said no.

You avoided the words

s u i c i d e

and

k i l l y o u r s e l f

and

s e l f h a r m

as if it's the words that were going to k i l l me.

I've thought about it.

I've thought about all of it.

s e l f h a r m

and

s u i c i d e.

What it would feel like.

How much it would hurt.

If it was true that it distracts you from your mind's pain.

If anyone would care,

If I would tell anyone for that matter.

I tried once.

s e l f h a r m.

I didn't do it.

It was as if my mind and body stopped me.

As if, for once,

They united to stop me hurting myself.

Normally, they go out of their way to make my eyes sting,

As my mind weeps,

When I realise that my body really is over 90% water,

Well was,

My tears always seemed endless.

-I don't know who I am without a bad mental health.

I don't know if I want to.

I don't want to be so envious of myself that I fall even deeper under the spell of mental illness.

It feels so strange calling myself mentally ill.

I was unsure if I should write it.

But an eating disorder is a mental illness,

So, I am mentally ill.

I don't think I like that label.

I don't know if I want to meet a mentally stable and healthy version of me.

I think I would hate her.

I would be so jealous,

And sad,

And angry.

That I-

I don't think I'd be able to cope.

The thought of her would completely take over my mind.

Quite ironic really,

That a healthy version of myself,

Would make me less stable.

-Mantras dress my mirror,

Little cards with 'inspirational' words stuck onto my reflection with a slither of Sellotape.

They are supposed to make me love myself.

Make me 'remember' my worth,

Like I ever knew I had any.

-I used to cry so loudly,

That I could be heard from downstairs.

Now I've learnt my lesson,

And when I cry,

I'm so silent, I can't be heard by someone in the same room.

-Everyone thinks they know me,

They know my smile,

And my laugh,

My frustration,

And disappointment,

But they do not *know* me.

They don't know my cry,

Or how most of what I tell them is a lie.

They do not know what I write,

Or the everyday battles that I fight.

They don't know of the pressure,

Forced upon me when we're together.

Everyone always thinks they know me,

But they do not *know* a thing.

-I don't eat breakfast anymore.

Not because I'm worried about my weight,

Although that used to be why,

I just don't want to.

I don't want to do much anymore.

Just like how I don't want to get out of bed.

I normally like a lay-in, who doesn't,

But I don't mean like that.

I mean I never want to leave,

I don't even want to sleep for any longer.

I just want to lay,

In silence.

-I don't know how I feel,

I'm not smiling.

I'm not laughing.

I'm not crying.

I'm not shouting,

Or screaming.

I'm not sad.

I'm not angry.

I'm not happy.

I'm not frustrated,

Or annoyed.

I can't feel anything.

I feel numb.

-You asked me if I am okay,

I said, 'fine'.

You believed me.

You asked me what's wrong,

I said, 'nothing'.

You believed me.

You asked me how my day was,

I said, 'good'.

And you believed me.

You believed every word.

Thinking that I felt heard, you left me alone.

How could you not see?

-As I look up in the sky,

I see nothing but grey

And hear nothing but rain.

Like the foggy clouds in my brain

And the ocean behind my eyes

That drowns my rose covered cheeks

Every time that I cry.

I see nothing but dark silhouettes of houses and trees,

Like the ghost town in my mind,

Nothing but spiritless souls to be found.

Looking through the rectangle glass in front of me,

I have nothing to say.

I just feel connected to the rainy day.

-I often think about my future.

Marriage,

Children,

Love.

I often wonder if ill have any of them,

If I'll ever be married,

And if I do, is it to someone I love?

Will we have children?

Will I ever even be loved?

I think about this when I see my friends,

And their thin silhouettes

And their even thinner bodies,

Their thighs, which have gaps

Their hairless skin

And defined faces.

I think about this when I eat.

I wonder if I should stop,

But it's me wondering,

And worrying

That makes me force food into my mouth,

And chew,

And swallow,

And, then regret.

I also think about this,

On every other occasion.

Before I shut my eyes to sleep,

When I wake up,

When I endlessly scroll through Insta,

I think about this when I look in the mirror,

And see the roundness of my face,

My disappearing chin,

My gapless thighs,

The hair on my legs that I missed when I shaved
last,

This is when it most bothers me,

When my worries,

Turn into something for me to see.

'A girl should be two things: who and what she wants to be.'

-Coco Chanel

-I am so fed up of crying.

It seems like the only thing I am capable to doing.

Crying,

And crying while writing about why I am crying.

-I am so tired,

I cannot think,

I cannot breathe.

My lungs, empty from my silent tears.

I feel empty.

I feel nothing.

I feel numb.

-I wish I could write happy poems.

The ones that inspire,

And make people smile.

I've tried.

I try.

My words always end up spiralling into the heaviness of my soul.

And the intensity of my mind.

-I should not be too scared to write because of you,

Or to share my poems because of you,

And your thoughts,

That you so blatantly and unnecessarily speak.

I should not be ashamed or anxious that my writing

And feelings

And thoughts

Don't match up to your time line,

Or perception of events,

That you were never involved in,

Or would never be involved in.

Writing is freeing,

And empowering,

I should not second guess every word I write because you replace my thoughts with anxiety,

And feelings of fraud,

Because you don't believe I feel,

I am not allowed to,

When I am around you.

f a m I l y

-I tell myself I'm not allowed to be anxious,

Or down,

Or upset.

I tell myself I have no right.

That there are people in the world who suffer a substantial amount more than me,

That I have no right to cry,

Me and my problems are nothing compared to other people.

-Sadness is like a drug,

It is so addicting.

One day spent in bed,

With my face consumed with the comfort of my pillow,

And my body warmly embraced by my unwashed bed sheets,

Turns into days,

Then weeks.

I think this is why I hate changing my bed.

I am so used to the feeling of my own tears,

And sadness,

And pain comforting me every morning,

And every night,

That I don't want to do it all again to make the new sheets feel the same.

-I think I am broken.

I don't want to do anything anymore.

I stay silent and stare unto the abys that is my ceiling or wall.

I have silent conversations with myself.

This all started happening when I was diagnosed

At first, I was thankful t identify my illness,

But now I am empty.

I think I might have broken myself.

-I've always been taught to avoid labels,

And when I say taught,

I mean I have learnt,

I observe and listen,

It is through that I have heard,

And it is through that I have learned.

Stray away from labels.

I hear the attacks behind peoples backs,

I hear how their thoughts and feelings are dismissed.

I have told three people about my diagnosis.

And I have always wanted to tall more people.

To be understood.

But I am too afraid,

So it is through my poems that I tell you.

The poems I never give you.

-I have vines on my stomach,

You know, the pink kind,

The ones that appear from excess body fat,

The ones I can barely look at,

The ones that are intensely carved into my skin,

The ones that consume me with guilt, whenever I touch my tummy,

They are growing like a disease spreads,

They 'bloomed' on my hips,

Now they have grown to my waist,

And now they are painting themselves onto my thighs too.

Are my legs their next victims?

I always used to tell myself they weren't that bad,

That out of all the flaws of my body,

They're not the worst,

But then, they were contained,

They peacefully rested on my skin then,

Now they devour my body,

I thought I could handle it,

I used to call them 'tiger stripes' in my older poems,

I'd make them seem somehow okay,

I'd make it seem like I accepted them,

Well, I guess I did, then.

-beauty

(noun). A combination of qualities that pleases the aesthetic senses, especially sight.

Why can't beauty be more than an appearance?

'Beauty is only skin deep. I think what's really important is finding a balance is body, mind and spirit'

-J Lo

-I hate my body.

And it is only now,

That I am on the verge of a breakdown I've been holding in for weeks,

That I realise it.

I've always known, but never like this.

My face sinks and mood drowns whenever I see a glimpse of myself,

My inconsistent self-love is really taking its toll.

I think it's making me resist love as a whole.

-I know that one day I will be better.

I will be fixed.

I know that one day I will be confident when I say that I am happy.

And I know that one day, I won't hate every millimetre of y body.

I can't wait for that day to come.

Btu, it just seems like I've been waiting for a long time.

-I wish I was the type of writer that-

Well, I wish I was the aesthetic writer,

The one that writes at coffee shops with a drink in hand,

Looking flawlessly beautiful as I casually write away.

Or the other type of writer I see on Instagram,

Who sits in fields or at the beach at sunset, or sunrise,

Again, looking flawlessly beautiful as they write,

Or even the type of writer, who actually writes,

I find that there's something so raw and natural about a poem or a story that has been written by hand.

I am the type of writer, who writes with hair straight from the company of my pillow,

In bed,

With my phone or laptop in hand,

My eyes either freshly awake,

Or forcing themselves not to close,

Wearing (every time) the same old joggers that my mum gave me,

Which are painted in the sequined words 'love sleep',

And have probably only seen the washing machine twice in it's life,

And with them, I either wear a matching, baggy grey jumper,

Or a bed top I pulled from my wardrobe.

What can I say, maybe I am an 'aesthetic writer'.

Although, sometimes, I do like to sit outside and write,

But only if it's a summer night.

I probably could be an aesthetic writer,

Who knows, it might even make my poems better,

But I can never force myself to write.

If I do, the poem either turns out horrible,

Or I can't write one at all.

That's why I say that poetry is often my therapy,

I write when I need to write.

-I don't really know who I am.

I know myself,

In the way that I know how I'm going to react to certain situations,

And I know my personal preferences,

But I don't who I am in the sense that I don't know who I like.

Men?

Women?

I don't know how to feel or react when I'm asked

the question either.

I don't know.

I'm 14.

Should I know?

I think the real question is,

Even if I knew myself, in that way,

Would anyone even want to date me,

Or give me a second thought?

-I am a stranger to myself,

When I look in the mirror,

I don't see me,

I see a girl in a cage,

Mental health worsening with age,

She shakes on the bars,

Wanting to be free,

She looks just like me.

I have an image in my head of what I looked like before 'it' took over.

'it'.

Body image,

Stereotypes,

Makeup,

And the makeup wipes that gave me pimples,

And insecurities about my dimples,

Weight gain that led to my minds pain,

A lack of 'good' friends,

And social media trends.

All of this led to my downfall,

And it is all of this that post-pone's my uprising.

-I remember the first and only time I liked my smile.

I was on the phone to my dad,

Talking about how, 'I think I'm finally accepting my eating disorder'.

'And myself'.

As my smiling lips moved more and more frantically with my words of happiness and hope,

I looked in the mirror,

By accident.

And for a second,

I paused and looked at myself smile,

It felt like all the pain, and hurt, was worthwhile.

I couldn't stop looking,

A tsunami of emotions consumed me,

Happiness,

Shock,

Love.

It only lasted for about a week.

I wouldn't cover my mouth while I smiled,

Or look away so that no one could see the devilish expression on my face.

In fact,

I smiled more.

Confident that one of my biggest past insecurities was a waste of time.

I felt love.

That was the first time I felt love for myself for a long time.

Maybe even the first time I've ever felt love for myself.

I hope I never forget that.

No matter how short of a time it lasted,

I was happy.

That's worth it.

Happiness.

-I always used to wish that my face could be a filter,

That I could scroll through all the snapchat filters,

Pick the one that made me look the prettiest,

And always have it.

But, I realised,

For the filter to work, it has to recognise a face,

Your face is the foundation,

The face you call pretty when you stare at your phone screen on snapchat,

Is the same face you bully,

And attack,

Every day when you look in the mirror,

Or see your reflection.

What your younger self say?

Why hurt yourself because of what others might think,

When self-love is more than enough?

I cannot wait for the day you realise that.

-'Wear your heart on your sleeve'.

One day I hope to wear all of me on my sleeve,

My heart,

My scars,

My wounds,

My fears,

My memories,

My happiness,

And sadness,

My growth,

My achievements,

My failures

And heartbreaks.

All of this is me,

My past, present and my future,

Accepting all of this is what'll set me free.

-Divinity is within the clouds,

So is tranquillity and immunity from pain.

In the clouds, you can breathe,

And relieve your shoulders of the world,

Because in the clouds, you're flying,

There is no crying,

Or trying too hard,

And there is no relying on yourself or others,

Because in the clouds you're free,

No longer barred behind the cage door of your own mind.

In the clouds, there are no dreams,

Just beams of hope that for one more day,

You might be able to cope.

My head is not stuck in the clouds,

I just don't want to leave them.

-Fabulous

And

Talented

Fantastic

Aspirational

Thoughtful

Free

And

Trustworthy

'Fat' is only an unpleasant word if you connote it with unpleasant things.

'I'm not going to conform, and hurt myself, and do something crazy to be a size 2'

-Amber Riley

-You know, strangely enough,

I think I am beginning to like myself again.

I find my stretch marks pretty,

I like how they stretch along my tummy,

As if they are hugging me,

I like my eyes,

And their colour,

And I like my eyelashes.

I like how my hair looks when it is straight out the shower,

I like my thighs,

And how they jiggle,

I like how, in some clothes,

My waist looks a bit smaller,

And I like how, from the front, I don't mind my tummy.

This is so weird.

I have never felt so at home with myself.

I like it.

I really like it.

-I don't care what you think anymore,

Or what you have to say,

About my arms at least.

You see, the thing is,

Frankly, I can't be bothered to shave every week,

Not anymore,

I'm fed up with razer rash consuming my body,

All because I don't want to be hairy,

You can keep telling me to shave,

I don't care anymore,

And it is so freeing to say it.

If I told you to shave your arms and legs,

Let's be honest, every hair on your body except the hair on your head,

Would you do it?

My arms are only hairier because I used to shave them.

Because my friend did, so I did,

And oh my god do I regret it.

I only shaved because I 'had' to,

Because my naïve self thought that pleasing you,

And everyone else that judges me,

Would make me a 'better' person.

Would make me more popular,

Would make me more accepted.

But, in reality it just made me more like you.

And anyway,

I've learnt now, that my skin is my home,

It protects me,

So I should protect it,

And I'm not going to strip it of its warmth,

Well, not as much as I used to.

So, kindly,

No, and I don't care.

'Make peace with your past so it won't screw up the present'

-Regina Brett

-Accept your past, present and future.

No matter how much you have been through,

Or will go through,

Without it all,

You could not possibly be you.

Dear Readers:

You reached the end! Thankyou for patience. If you are struggling, know that this is not the end. One day, no matter how soon or far away that day is for you, you will overcome this. And that day is worth waiting and fighting for. You're worthy of help, and love, and kindness and everything that's good in the world. Trust me.

Hopefully, we can reunite when I publish my next book, and hopefully, that book will be happier.

Dear reader, I tried to write a poem for you, I asked for you to love yourself no matter how much you struggle with your mental, or like me are a bit temperamental. I hoped that you would learn from this book to love yourself, not because it is full of inspiring poems, because it isn't, but because you learn from my pain, that your own pain isn't worth feeling, it isn't worth your time, that you should just focus on healing. I tried to write a poem for you, I struggled and gave up, you reading this book, full of my own vulnerability, and pain, is enough for me to become speechless. Thankyou reader, we have come this far together. You know more about me now than my mum or dad, that's actually pretty weird now that I think about it. Anyway, say thankyou with me, to everyone who has hurt you, and to everyone who will hurt you, to everyone who has healed you, and to everyone that will heal you. Without all of these people, no matter how much you might love or hate them, without them, you would probably not be the person you are (yes, I know it's cringey). Thankyou my dear reader, lots of love xx

The next few pages are yours, write with your heart, and rhyme with your soul...

Quick Acknowledgements

I want to say thankyou to all the people that have hurt me and affected me in some way, because without you, I wouldn't have written the majority of these poems. Thankyou.

Thanks to the family members that supported me, and to my uncle Matt (who is also a poet) for initially inspiring me to publish, and for publishing my poem 'What is femininity?' in his book. Also, my aunty Jo for being really supportive and helping during a difficult time.

Thanks to my dad, for publishing the book, and supporting me through the process of writing the manuscript, and for encouraging to be more confident with myself and my poems.

Thanks to the English teachers who cheered me on, encouraged me to write and publish, thank you!

Thanks to Red Medusa too, for encouraging me to write and publish, inspiring me and for keeping in contact with me when I was writing the manuscript.

And lastly, thanks to the poets of TikTok and Instagram who inspired me.

-Thankyou! X

Why I wrote Dear Diary

-My original goal for Dear Diary was to make myself proud, and become more confident within myself and what I write, however, during the time I was writing, I became more aware of the mental illness, and general influx of bad mental health in society. This made me want to write for others as well as myself.

My goal now for Dear Diary, is to reach young people and teenagers such as myself, who are struggling with mental health and mental illness. From my own experiences with having a bad mental health, I found that reading poems from others who feel or have felt the same, was more impactful than inspiring poetry from a healthy mind, because of this, my goal for the book is to reach young people, and preach that loneliness is not never-ending, through the use of my own experiences.

Mental health is so important, and so is every mind.

What is ARFID?

-ARFID is an eating disorder common among adolescents.

-It stands for Avoidant Restrictive Food Intake Disorder.

-ARFID is an extreme fear of 'new' or 'fear' foods. Interaction with these foods can lead to panic attacks, hyperventilation, nausea and more.

-ARFID varies between person, but commonly, the person with ARFID experiences the symptoms listed above when interacting with foods outside of their 'safe' group of foods.

-ARFID fears and symptoms can vary from an extreme fear of trying new foods, fearing illness, death etc if you eat a 'fear food' and more.

-ARFID can lead to nutritional deficiencies and in severe cases, hospitalisation as it can be a deadly illness.

If you want to understand more about ARFID and other eating disorders I recommend doing some research. It is important that everyone in society Is aware of eating disorders, how they begin, how they can be treated and how to help yourself or others with an eating disorder.

A useful website to visit would be ARFID Awareness UK.

The Emily Project is also a beautiful program, aiming to help people overcome and treat eating disorders, food issues and body image.

(As of December 2022)

My collection of books:

-How sunflowers bloom under moonlight- Isabella Dorta

-A poetry book for sad messed up teenagers- Gracie Adams

-It gets better b*tch-Gracie Adams

-Dear Girl-Aija Mayrock

-The sun will rise and so will we-Jennae Cecilia

-Milk and honey-Rupi Kaur

-The sun and her flowers-Rupi Kaur

-Home body-Rupi Kaur

-Breathing water-Red Medusa

-The witch doesn't burn in this one-Amanda Lovelace

Help Page:

-BEAT- 0808 801 0677

-YoungMinds

-Childline- 0800 1111

-Bullying UK

-Kooth- 0300 304 5555

-The MIX- 0808 808 4994

-Good Thinking- 0800 068 41 41

Never feel like you are not worthy of help, you are worthy, and you deserve help.

All numbers and charities are as of December 2022

"You can dream and plan for a healthy, happy future, but that's no good if you're struggling in the present."

-Me

<u>Socials (as of December 2022):</u>

-Instagram -> lollawright_poet

-TikTok -> lollawright_poet

Thankyou!

Printed in Great Britain
by Amazon

15972551R00064